I0503390

Big Innovation Roadmap:
Big Picture and Big Change

Ernest L. Hughes, Ed.D.

Copyright © 2015 Ernest L. Hughes

All rights reserved.

ISBN: 1516901479
ISBN-13: 978-1516901470

DEDICATION

This book is dedicated to the volunteers, professionals and social entrepreneurs who work to improve the quality of life of all those affected by hunger, homelessness, and mental ill-health through advocacy, education, and support. In the spirit of Conscious Capitalism®, the profits from the sale of this book will be donated to projects and organizations that support this mission.

CONTENTS

ACKNOWLEDGMENTS

CHANGE PLUS™ is a trademark of HughesGlobal, LLC.

Conscious Capitalism® is a registered trademark of Conscious Capitalism, Inc.

Customer-in-Center is a trademark of Gautam Mahajan.

Lean Coffee is a trademark of Modus Operandi.

1 INTRODUCTION

"Everything you see around you was once an idea."
Kobi Yamada ⑬

The toughest sales job for anyone, according to a recent research paper, "is to sell their own company on new ideas and opportunities."③ Even successful organizations, filled with sensible people and led by smart managers can have difficulty with innovation and change. ⑫

This book explores a hypothetical Big Innovation Roadmap for increasing the adoption and scaling the practice of innovation across the enterprise in order to accelerate the creation, capture, and retention of value for an organization's stakeholders. Strategies for negotiating the right path and working together to effect innovation and change are discussed. Applied research, trends and cases in Big Innovation are also examined. These findings are the result of ongoing applied research programs on Big Innovation and Big Change, and two recent workshops on becoming a more innovative organization.

The book contains nine chapters. Chapter 2 is a brief overview of the CHANGE PLUS™ service utilized to produce the roadmap. Chapter 3 contains and explains the Big Innovation Roadmap. Chapter 4 outlines strategies for the right path, and Chapter 5 summarizes the research and trends. Three learning aids are presented in Chapters 6 through 8 – Cases, a Retrospective form, and a table of Useful Definitions.

The book concludes with a select list of useful articles and books in Chapter 9, and a list of useful web resources in Chapter 10. Some of these are referenced by number throughout the book as ① or ❶ respectively.

2 CHANGE PLUS™

The Big Innovation Roadmap was created using the CHANGE PLUS™ service offered by HughesGlobal, LLC. This service creates change roadmaps utilizing a variety of development, design, evaluation, and change processes and recipes resulting in five plans:

1. Case for Change,
2. Communication,
3. Learning,
4. Transition, and
5. Sustainability.

Innovation Agents facilitate dialogue and conversation via action learning and collaborative coaching to develop these plans.

3 BIG INNOVATION ROADMAP

This chapter describes and presents a hypothetical high-level conceptual model—a Big Innovation Roadmap (Figure 1), for expanding and scaling innovation across the enterprise in order to accelerate the creation, capture, and retention of value for an organization's stakeholders.

There are many definitions for the concept of innovation. Generally, "execution of new ideas that create business value" will be used as the definition throughout this book unless otherwise defined. Several others are listed in the Useful Definitions chapter.

As an organization seeks to expand and scale innovation practices, it will need to decide that innovation is a competitive differentiator, and create idea and innovation management structures such as Portfolio Management, Communities of Practice (CoPs), and Enterprise Change Management. Systems like Attensa and Ideascale will also be needed. ❶ ❹

Dr. J. Juran reminds us of the importance of overcoming individual, organizational, and cultural resistance to change in such improvement efforts. Regular conversations, facilitated by Innovation Agents, are needed to overcome such resistance. Lean Coffee and Customer Circles are two conversation methods that can be utilized to do so.

Increased value results when innovation practices move within and across teams and functional departments, then beyond organizational boundaries into value chains and innovation networks (COINs).

Leadership agility is required to make these transitions happen.

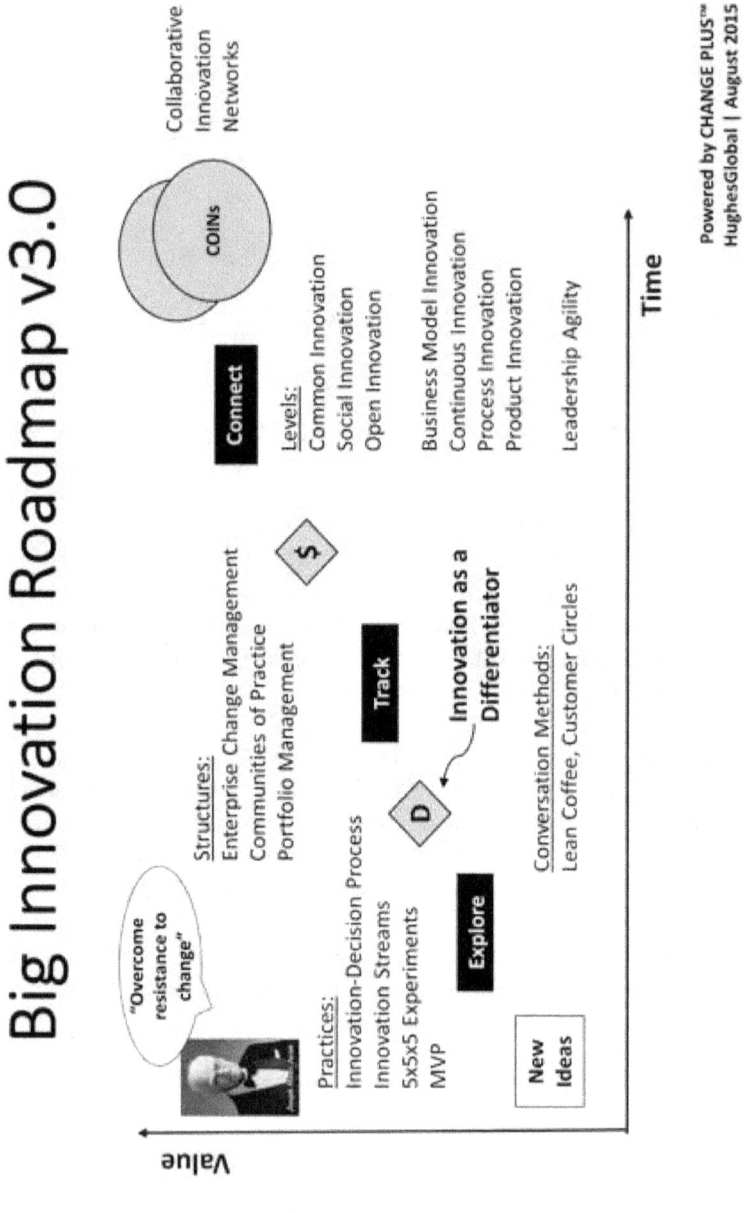

Big Innovation Roadmap v3.0

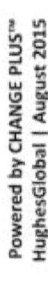

Value

"Overcome resistance to change"

New Ideas

Explore

Practices:
Innovation-Decision Process
Innovation Streams
5x5x5 Experiments
MVP

Conversation Methods:
Lean Coffee, Customer Circles

D

Track

Innovation as a Differentiator

Structures:
Enterprise Change Management
Communities of Practice
Portfolio Management

$

Connect

Levels:
Common Innovation
Social Innovation
Open Innovation

Business Model Innovation
Continuous Innovation
Process Innovation
Product Innovation

Leadership Agility

COINs

Collaborative Innovation Networks

Time

Powered by CHANGE PLUS™
HughesGlobal | August 2015

Figure 1. Big Innovation Roadmap

4 STRATEGIES

Strategies for negotiating the right path an working together to effect innovation and change are discussed in this chapter.

Rogers' Innovation-Decision Process is a widely accepted and adopted model for innovation. In this process, adopting an innovation is a two-phase, five-stage process (Figure 2). In the first phase, individuals gather information and form opinions about a possible innovation. The three stages in this phase are Knowledge, Persuasion, and Decision. In the second phase, the innovation is implemented and confirmation about the adoption decision is sought.

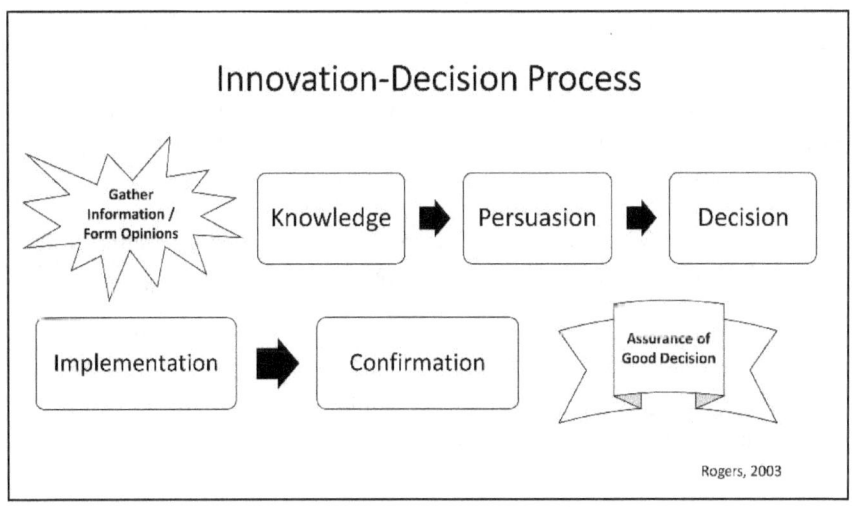

Figure 2. Innovation-Decision Process ⑨

According to this model, an individual at the Knowledge stage is exposed to an innovation and gains understanding of it. At the Persuasion stage, an individual forms an attitude toward the innovation – either favorable or unfavorable. In the Decision stage, an individual makes a choice to adopt or reject the innovation. Note that an individual doesn't always have a choice. An individual uses the innovation in the Implementation stage and seeks reinforcement of their adoption decision in the Confirmation stage. Additionally, a previous decision to adopt or reject the innovation could also be reversed at this stage.

At the organizational level, Tushman & O'Reilly recommend developing and utilizing three innovation streams concurrently to create more value. ⑫

The Incremental Stream are innovations that are small extensions of existing technology. The Architectural Stream are innovations that are reinventions of existing technology. The Discontinuous Stream are innovations that are totally new approaches to satisfying a market need.

Developing and managing these streams is not straightforward. Sustained success requires building strong organizational capabilities, structures, competencies, and cultures. A strong strategic management process enables that. Additionally, organizational leaders must encourage discontinuous organizational change.

Schrage describes a process, called 5x5x5 Experiments, that can be utilized to fill the innovation streams.⑩

In this approach, 5 teams of 5 people have 5 days to come up with a portfolio of 5 business experiments that should take no longer than 5 weeks to run and cost no more than $5,000 each to conduct.

Each experiment is supported by a business case. The experiments should be simple, fast, and cheap with compelling results. Schrage emphasizes that the main result of conducting 5x5x5 experiments is more effective innovators.

Similarly, Reis recommends building a "Minimum Viable Product" (MVP) with limited features to test an idea directly with intended customers.⑧

Examples of an MVP include a smoke test, mockup, prototype, simulation, or video. Innovators should learn and "pivot" as needed from the feedback they receive.

Ideas, and support for them, are advanced in an organization through conversation. Lean Coffee and Customer Circles are two useful conversation methods to do so.

Lean Coffee is an agenda-free, semi-structured meeting format styled after Lean Kanban techniques. First, a Kanban with three columns is setup – To Discuss, Discussing, and Discussed. Participants next write on notes what they what to discuss, then multi-vote (typically two votes) about which topics are important to them. Notes flow through the columns as the conversation unfolds.❻

Customer Circles are much more formal. They are an organization-sponsored group of frontline employees, a few managers, and support people who focus on the customer. Typically, Customer Circles are coordinated by the Chief Customer Officer, and no customers are actually involved. Members of the Customer Circle try to determine what makes customers happy and unhappy, develop Customers' Do Not Annoy (DNA) Factors, Delight Factors and Bill of Rights, and implement a Customer Improvement Program with Customer-in-Center processes.⑤

Manns & Rising, building upon the Innovation-Decision Process, developed a set of useful and practical communication patterns or recipes for individuals to use to make their idea happen. These patterns are organized into four categories: Strategize, Share Information and Seek Help, Inspire Others, and Target Resistance. Specific patterns to Target Resistance include: Pick Your Battles, Wake-Up Call, Myth Buster, and Easier Path.⑥

Howell determined the characteristics and behaviors of effective champions for innovation and change.

Characteristics	Behaviors

• Breadth of interest
  • Broad general knowledge
  • Experience in a wide range of domains
  • Diverse interests
  • Seek information
	• Conveying confidence and enthusiasm about the innovation
	• Enlist support and involvement of key stakeholders
	• Persist in the face of adversity

from different domains
 • Flexible role orientation
    • Keep own knowledge and skills up-to-date
    • Keep well informed about issues
    • Develop and make recommendations concerning issues affecting the organization
    • Immerse themselves in business units outside of their own unit
    • Seek problems to work on from their network of relationships
	• Rely on personal networks inside and outside the organization
	 • Scout widely for new ideas and opportunities
	 • Analyze key stakeholders' interests
	 • Tailor their selling strategies to be maximally persuasive
	 • Tie innovations to positive organizational outcomes

Figure 3. Effective Champions ③

Innovation and Change Champions are often required to surmount the impediments and "innovation killers" of what Gaynor calls the "Virtual Innovation Prevention Department" (VIPD) that most organizations have. Frequent occupants of the VIPD include CEOs, other executives, managers, fellow innovators, and peers and colleagues of innovators.

Innovation Killers include:

1. Undetermined or vague strategies,
2. Conflicting priorities,
3. Leadership style that is too top-down or too laissez-faire,
4. Ineffective executive management team,
5. Undeveloped middle management,
6. Absence of business-oriented professionals in all disciplines,
7. Lack of trust, and
8. Inadequate open communication.

A key role of the VIPD, according to Gaynor, is to resist change.②

Feit developed a constrained, systematic search method for discovering ideas and opportunities beyond alertness and luck.① Constrained, Systematic Search is a multi-stage model for how innovators can mine a promising set of known information channels, called a Consideration Set, to search information channels for signals, interpret feedback, and discover ideas. Business Intelligence tools like Attensa can help do this.❶

Feit's FVRI Framework can be utilized to measure and predict the wealth creation of an innovation. FVRI stands for the attributes of the innovation: Fit, Value, Rarity, and Inimitability.

Kim & Mauborgne defined three useful tools for evaluating a new business product. These are: (1) Develop a Buyer Utility Map; (2) Set Strategic Price, and (3) Build a Profitable Business Model.④

A Buyer Utility Map determines the location of a new product versus existing products along two dimensions: Stages of Buyer Experience Cycle, and Utility Levers. Stages are: Purchase, Delivery, Use, Supplements, Maintenance, and Disposal. Levers are Environmental Friendliness, Fun and Image, Risk, Convenience, Simplicity, and Customer Productivity.

Setting Strategic Price is a two-step process. Step one is to identify the price of competitive products that captures the largest groups of customers, called the "price corridor of the mass." Step two is to determine a price level within the corridor based upon the degree of legal and resource protection available for the new product, and the ability of competitors to imitate it.

Building a Profitable Business Model entails determining a pricing model for the new product along with cost targets and potential sourcing partners. Potential adoption hurdles—resistance to change, by employees, business partners, and consumers must also be addressed.

Idea and Innovation metrics can be useful. Some organizations simply count the number of new ideas and their adoption on a monthly basis. More sophisticated metrics include Innovation Pipeline Strength and Return on Innovation. IPS = sum (Innovation Projects x Future Revenue Potential). ROI = [(Net profit from new products & services) − (Innovation costs for these products & services)]/(Innovation costs for these products & services.

Ideascale is a system to enable all of this. It utilizes a crowdsourcing model. Users submit their ideas and Champions support them as teams develop proposals to be evaluated by Experts. Management approves and then allocates resources. ❹

5 RESEARCH & TRENDS

Applied research, case studies, and emerging trends in Big Innovation are examined in this chapter.

Here are some notable findings from research on innovation:

1. There is no magic formula for innovation.

2. Change is a requirement for innovation.

3. Trust is a key ingredient of innovation.

4. Address innovation systematically.

5. Innovativeness may be related to personality. ❺

6. How an innovation is classified may determine what organizational resources are allocated to develop it.

7. Gartner recommends choosing a specific business focus and time frame for ideas, engaging employees first, then extending to customers and partners. ❸

8. Successful innovation depends upon successful management innovation – changes in organizational structure, management processes, and practices.

9. Internal change agents are key to management innovation. In large organizations, transformational leadership may also be required. The CEO often may fill, or is expected to fill, this role.

10. Resistance to new ideas and change may be due to competing

commitments.

Here are some notable results from studies on trends in innovation:

1. Innovation powered by entrepreneurship is an important factor in prosperity and wealth creation. ⑦ ⑪

2. Innovation is increasingly considered to be a key driver of an organization's long term success.

3. Innovation is increasingly distributed beyond a single organization to stakeholders in its value chain.

4. Prominent organizations are staffing internal Innovation Manager or Consultant positions. Typically, these organizations emphasize Project Management skills.

5. Change agents are evolving to become Innovation agents.

6 CASES

Here are two cases. Utilize the Big Innovation Roadmap concepts, strategies, and practices along with your own knowledge and experience to answer the big question. Share your response at the corresponding post on the HughesGlobal blog, http://www.hughesglobal.com/blog.

#	Case
1	**Pay it Forward Pizza** https://www.youtube.com/watch?v=brzjeICcIt0 **Big Question: What would it take for the large pizza chains or other food service providers to adopt this idea?** ❽
2	**No PATH for the S.T.Eye Condom** Detecting STIs, http://www.cnn.com/2015/06/24/health/condoms-change-color/ Color-Changing Condoms Proposed to Detect Sexual Infection, http://www.dezeen.com/2015/06/24/colour-changing-condom-concept-detect-sti-sexually-transmitted-infection/ Teens Think Up Clever Condoms, http://www.washingtonpost.com/news/morning-mix/wp/2015/06/24/teens-invent-clever-condoms-that-change-colors-to-indicate-std-exposure/

'Glowing' condoms could tell if you have an STI,
http://www.dailymail.co.uk/sciencetech/article-3135833/Glowing-condoms-soon-reveal-STI-Students-design-smart-contraceptive-detect-disease.html

Are condoms that detect STIs and change color a good idea?,
http://www.path.org/blog/2015/08/friday-think-color-condoms/

No, teenagers did not invent STI-detecting color-changing condoms,
http://www.hopesandfears.com/hopes/future/science/214641-tabloids-invent-teenagers-inventing-sti-detecting-condoms

Maker of Sexually Transmitted Disease Test win Business Plan Competition, http://www.geekwire.com/2015/maker-of-sexually-transmitted-disease-test-wins-uw-business-plan-competition/

Big Question: What would it take for PATH to get behind this idea? ➐

7 RETROSPECTIVE

Use this form to define goals for your innovation journey. Consider individual, team, organization, and value chain levels. What are you going to do more of (+)? What are your going to do less of (-)? Share with your innovators and innovation networks (COINS & CoPs).

+	-

8 USEFUL DEFINITIONS

Here is a list of useful definitions.

Term / Concept	Definition
Absorptive Capacity	Organizational capabilities for managing and assimilating knowledge and applying it to commercial ends
Agility	Continual readiness to change
Best practice	A practice that is performed in a superior way
COINs	Collaborative Innovation Networks
CoPs	Communities of Practice
Crowdsourcing	"Crowd" of users
DNA	Do Not Annoy
ECM	Enterprise Change Management
FVRI Framework	Fit, Value, Rarity, Inimitability
Green Tomato	Potential to develop lies ahead
Impediment	Anything that obstructs the smooth flow of work
Innovation	1. Useful improvements in existing technologies, ideas, processes, products, or services 2. Execution of new ideas that create business value 3. Creative destruction 4. The successful exploitation of new ideas
IWG	Innovation Working Group
KAI	Kirton Adaption-Innovation Inventory
MVP	Minimum Viable Product
VIPD	Virtual Innovation Prevention Department

9 RESOURCES

Here is a select list of useful resources.

① Fiet, J. (2008). *Prescriptive entrepreneurship*. Northampton, MA: Edward Elgar.

② Gaynor, G. (2002). *Innovation by design: What it takes to keep your company on the cutting edge*. New York: AMACOM.

③ Howell, J. (2005). The right stuff: Identifying and developing effective champions of innovation. *Academy of Management Executive*, 19(2), 108-119.

④ Kim, W.C.. & Mauborgne, R. (2000, September-October). Knowing a winning business idea when you see one. *Harvard Business Review*.

⑤ Mahajan, G. (2010). *Total customer value management: Transforming business thinking*. New Delhi: Sage Publications.

⑥ Manns, M., & Rising, L. (2015). *More fearless change: Strategies for making your ideas happen*. Boston, MA: Addison-Wesley Professional.

⑦ Phelps, E. (2013). *Mass flourishing: How grassroots innovation created jobs, challenge, and change*. Princeton, NJ: Princeton University Press.

⑧ Reis, E. (2011). *The lean startup: How today's entrepreneurs use continuous innovation to create radically successful businesses*. New York: Crown Business.

⑨ Rogers, E. (2003). *Diffusion of innovations*, 5th edition. New York: Free Press.

⑩ Schrage, M. (2014). *The innovator's hypothesis: How cheap experiments are worth more than good ideas*. Cambridge, MA: MIT Press.

⑪ Swann, G. (2012). *Common innovation: How we create the wealth of nations*. Northampton, MA: Edward Elgar Publishing.

⑫ Tushman, M., & O'Reilly, III, C. (1997). *Winning through innovation: A practical guide to leading organizational change and renewal*. Cambridge, MA: Harvard Business School Press.

⑬ Yamada, K. (2014). *What do you do with an idea?* Compendium, Inc.

Additional related resources are available at the HughesGlobal Bookstore, http://www.hughesglobal.com/resources.

10 WEB RESOURCES

Here is a select list of useful web resources.

❶ Attensa, http://attensa.com

❷ Enterprise Change Management,
    http://www.prosci.com/ecm1/overview/

❸ Gartner, http://www.gartner.com

❹ Ideascale, http://ideascale.com/

❺ Kirton Adaption-Innovation Inventory, http://www.kaicentre.com/

❻ Lean Coffee, http://leancoffee.org/

❼ Rosa's Fresh Pizza, http://www.rosasfreshpizza.com/

ABOUT THE AUTHOR

Ernest L. Hughes ("Ernie" or "Lincoln") is a Senior Management Consultant, Business Coach, and Managing Partner of HughesGlobal, LLC, his consulting and education network focused on helping individuals, teams, organizations, and value chains realize their potential and flourish through leadership development and organizational learning. He is also an Associate Professor in the School of Business for American Public University System, an Adjunct Professor in Information Systems Management at Seattle Pacific University, and a part-time Lecturer for Executive Education for the University of Washington Bothell.

Prior to launching is consulting and education network, Hughes enjoyed broad leadership responsibility in a range of organizations for more than thirty years. He was most recently Director of Technical Services for Recreational Equipment, Inc. Before joining REI, Hughes was co-founder, Chief Information Officer and Director of Information & Learning Systems & Technology for Cascadia College after a fifteen-year technology career with Boeing. At Boeing, he managed business applications, systems engineering, application architecture, software process improvement, software cost management, software engineering education, and merger integration functions and programs. He started his career as a software developer.

Hughes earned a Master of Science degree in Global Supply Chain Management from the University of Alaska Anchorage, A Doctorate in Educational Leadership and a Masters in Software Engineering from Seattle University, a MBA from the California State University, Bakersfield, an a Bachelor of Science degree in Computer Science from California Polytechnic University, San Luis Obispo. He has training and certification in a number of specialties, including organizational excellence from ASQ, entrepreneurship from the Kauffman Foundation, and change management from Prosci.

www.ingramcontent.com/pod-product-compliance
Lightning Source LLC
Chambersburg PA
CBHW070928180526
45168CB00005B/2192

* 9 7 8 1 5 1 6 9 0 1 4 7 0 *